VICTORIA AND

A HISTORY OF THE

ENGLISH

OFFICE

1951

FOREWORD

This history of the English Chair has been prepared by Mr. Ralph Edwards, Keeper of the Department of Woodwork, and is illustrated by more than a hundred examples from the Museum collections, covering the collection from about 1500 to the end of the Georgian period. Chairs in the late Stuart and neo-classic styles have until recently been inadequately represented, but the acquisition of the contents of Ham House and Osterley Park have transformed the position in that respect.

LEIGH ASHTON,
Director

Victoria & Albert Museum

October 1950

THOUGH movable chairs were certainly known in England before the Norman Conquest, throughout the Middle Ages, even in royal palaces and the castles of great nobles they remained comparatively scarce.[1] Settles, benches and stools were the ordinary seats, while chairs were regarded as symbols of authority reserved for the master of the house and distinguished guests: this symbolic significance long continued to attach to them, and is still commemorated by the term "Chairman" for the person who takes his place at the head of a board. Down to early Georgian times a rigorous etiquette governed the use of chairs on ceremonial occasions at Court.

In medieval illuminated manuscripts throne-like structures resembling ecclesiastical stalls are sometimes shown standing against the walls in halls or chambers, with a "dosser" or backing of tapestry or embroidered material behind the occupant and a "banker" or cushion on the seat. A lighter variety often represented in illuminations (Fig. 1) was of X shape, a form which dates back to the early Middle Ages and was in use throughout Western Europe. References occur in inventories of the fifteenth century to "Flaunders chairs" (part of a large traffic in foreign furniture) and to others made *Ad Modum Anglicanum*, but such terse descriptions do not suffice to determine their character. Turned or "thrown" chairs are also found mentioned—a variety of great antiquity and wide geographical distribution which remained in favour until a much later date, the seats being triangular and the whole structure turned (Fig. 10). These were produced by the Turners, a trade guild whose existence can be traced from the beginning of the fourteenth century, though they did not obtain a charter of incorporation until 1604.[2]

The form of some of the earliest surviving domestic chairs shows them to have been evolved from the chest by the addition of a panelled back and sides. In the carving of Fig. 2 an important example of this small group of "box-chairs", the linen-fold pattern that figures so frequently in late Gothic woodwork is combined with ornament in which Renaissance influence can be clearly discerned.

A chair found in a Devonshire village about fifty years since (Fig. 3) is of the French type called *caquetoire* (*caqueter* to chatter) or *chaire de femme*, in allusion to the passion for gossip that is supposed to have popularised it. There are many chairs of this type in Continental collections (the Museum has two fine French examples)[3] exhibiting a considerable variety of design, but enquiry has failed to reveal the existence abroad of any close parallel. The blunt and summary handling of the foliated scrollwork and demi-terminal figures framing a woman's head in a lozenge, is characteristic of

West Country carving. Chairs of similar pattern were certainly produced in England (Fig. 5); while the close alliance of the French and Scotch Crowns at this period caused the form to be adopted in Scotland. Among these early "joyned" chairs should also be included the so-called "Glastonbury" type (based on North Italian models), in which the back has a pronounced rake and the arms, shaped underneath, slope upwards to support the elbows (Fig. 6).

For the building and equipment of his new palaces Henry VIII employed a number of foreign artists and craftsmen: through their influence, England was brought into closer touch with the Renaissance and the more advanced civilisation of the Continent. In the long lists of the king's possessions, drawn up after the accession of Edward VI (1547) many magnificent chairs are described, which, if not of foreign origin, were derived from French and Italian prototypes. Some were of walnut (a wood which now began to supplement the native oak) painted and gilded, while a number were of the traditional X shape with "pomells", or finials of gilt wood or copper. The frames of such chairs were completely covered with silk or velvet trimmed with fringes glued down and secured by ornamental gilt nails; the seats consisting of loose cushions supported on webbing between the side rails. An "X chair", of which the condition recalls the description "sore worne" in a contemporary inventory, is still preserved in Winchester Cathedral, and is said to have been used by Mary Tudor at her marriage to Philip of Spain: in their portraits the Queen and great courtiers are shown seated in chairs of this kind.[4] But such luxuries were in no way representative of the general standard of furnishing, and contemporary inventories prove that even in large houses chairs were still greatly outnumbered by stools.

The familiar panel-back type of joined chair came into general use towards the end of the sixteenth century. Made of oak and more rarely of walnut, they were sometimes inlaid in a variety of coloured wood (box, holly, bog-oak and sycamore being the favourites) with chequer patterns and conventional floral sprays. Massive at first, the construction became lighter as the evolution advanced, and in later specimens there is a tendency to florid enrichment; as in Fig. 9, where the back, cresting and framework are carved with a medley of foliated scrolls. There were local variations of the type, the treatment in Lancashire being particularly distinctive; while in Yorkshire and Derbyshire shortly before the Restoration another variety was introduced in which the space between the uprights is filled with an arcade of turned balusters supported on a central rail (Figs. 21 & 22).

Upholstered furniture was becoming plentiful in great houses about the end of Elizabeth's reign. Chairs of X form continued to be made but are now very rare owing to the perishable nature of the beechwood frames. An arm-chair of this form, covered with faded

6

velvet originally crimson and trimmed with tarnished gold fringe, once belonged to Archbishop Juxon, who, when Bishop of London, attended Charles I on the scaffold (Fig. 13). Among the magnificent furniture sold after the King's execution by the Council of State were a number of similar arm-chairs covered with velvet and cloth of silver, several being embroidered with the royal ccgnizances "ye armes of England holden by beastes".

In the early years of the seventeenth century, chairs with padded backs were made in sets without arms,[5] and were probably intended to accommodate the farthingale, or hooped skirt, which by then had attained extravagant dimensions. The Museum possesses two of these "farthingale chairs", still retaining their original coverings (Figs. 14 & 15). In an early upholstered arm-chair formerly at Boughton House, Northamptonshire (Fig. 16) the back, formed of a panel of velvet lined with leather and nailed to the uprights, is raised high above the seat rail, and the material is nailed down on the upper surfaces of the arms. At Knole Park, Sevenoaks, there are upholstered arm-chairs of far more elaborate character. Several are of X form and date from James I's reign, while others closely resemble French and Flemish examples and those represented in the engravings of domestic interiors by Abraham Bosse,[6] the arm-supports, legs and stretchers being completely covered with silk or velvet. Another variety, in favour under the Protectorate, seems to reflect the austerity of the times. The structure is composed of plain bars and knob turning (though a scrolled front stretcher anticipating later developments in transitional examples sometimes mitigated the severity of the design) (Fig. 23), the seats and back panels being upholstered in cow-hide fastened to the frame by brass-headed nails.

Soon after the return of Charles II and his court from exile the character of fashionable chairs was transformed, and a new type (already familiar in France and Holland) was introduced in which walnut was used in conjunction with caning for the first time. In early specimens the arms are flat and bowed, and uprights and stretchers are spirally turned, these members at the points of junction being morticed and tenoned into rectangular blocks (Fig. 30). Chairs of this kind, "turned all over" and admirable from the functional point of view, were soon superseded by another variety of which the ornate baroque character aptly expresses the spirit of the age. Scrolled forms were employed for arms and front legs, stretchers, cresting and back panel framing being now exploited as decorative areas. These members were pierced and lavishly carved. A crown supported by amorini (appropriate to the restored monarchy) is among the most familiar motives, but the craftsman's exuberant fancy was responsible for considerable variety in the ornament

7

employed. In a fine arm-chair (Fig. 33) a crowned female head decorates front stretcher and cresting, while amorini sport amid grape-laden branches below. These late Stuart chairs in some instances closely approximate Continental models, but in foreign examples the rope of the spiral turning is thicker, the hollows less prominent, the resulting twist being close and rapid. The ornament of imported chairs is generally more crisply cut, lighter in handling and in lower relief; while the stretcher between the back legs is often omitted. Beech stained to resemble walnut was employed for the cheaper varieties, though owing to its vulnerability to worm Evelyn would have liked to see its use prohibited.[7]

About 1690 a tendency becomes noticeable towards greater sobriety in design. The height of the back is increased, and through-out the structure there is a marked emphasis on vertical lines. The uprights and legs are of baluster form, and front stretcher and crest-ing are often composed of pierced scrolls symmetrically arranged. The ornate front stretcher was abandoned on certain models, and replaced by carved diagonal rails meeting in a central finial. As an alternative to carving, the space between the uprights was filled with pierced foliage and scroll-work. Some of these chairs, dating from William III's reign, recall designs by the celebrated Huguenot architect, Daniel Marot, who came over from Holland and spent several years here in the service of William III. In the attempt to produce a handsome chamber ornament rather than a serviceable seat sound principles of construction were sometimes sacrificed, socket and dowel being substituted for tenon and mortice as a means of attachment.

Many of these late Stuart chairs were japanned, a form of decoration for which at this period there was an avid demand. In a set of this kind at Ham House a naïve attempt has been made to reproduce an Oriental form. They bear the coronet of Elizabeth Dysart, Duchess of Lauderdale (Fig. 44) and are probably the set described in an inventory of 1683 as "12 back stooles with cane bottoms, japanned". Decorated with birds, figures and floral sprays on a dark green ground, where the surface has not been exposed to the sun, the japanned ornament still retains its polychromatic brilliance. "Cane chairs japanned" are often found entered in contemporary inventories, but on seat furniture such decoration was particularly perishable and very few genuine specimens have survived.

In the upholstered chairs which became fashionable soon after the Restoration the framework was of turned walnut; the backs were low and the arms were padded on their upper surfaces. About the middle of the reign a more luxurious type of "Easie" chair was introduced, damask, embroidered silk and figured Genoa velvets being employed for the coverings. In the Queen's Closet at Ham there are two winged chairs with iron ratchets to let down the backs which were made for the Duke and Duchess of Lauderdale, and are described in the '79 inventory as "two sleeping chayres carv'd and guilt frames covered with crimson and gould stuff". The scrolled front stretchers centre in amorini holding a bunch of grapes and the front legs rest on sea-horses (Fig. 39). Ham is plentifully supplied with upholstered chairs of this period all still retaining their original coverings, and a set (in the Withdrawing Room when the inventory was taken) are highly characteristic of the baroque splendours that caused the house equipped by Elizabeth Dysart to be regarded by contemporaries as a synonym for luxury (Fig. 40). The arms finish in dolphin's heads, and the legs and stretchers are carved with the interlaced bodies of the fish, gilding and colour being combined in the enrichment. In the inventory the set is described as consisting of "6 arm chairs, 6 back stools, carved and gilt covered with rich brocade"; and this pink and yellow brocaded satin is largely responsible for the opulent effect. Here the fringes are straight, but on other easy chairs of the period such trimmings are tasselled and elaborately festooned. The accounts of the Lord Chamberlain's Department and the Warrants issued by the Master of the Great Wardrobe throw valuable light on the evolution of style and on the activities of the craftsmen who made furniture for the Crown. At this time they afford some evidence of specialisation. For example, in the output of Thomas Roberts, who supplied a quantity of fine furniture for Chatsworth and the Royal palaces under William III, chairs figure prominently, while early in George I's reign Richard Roberts, probably his son, is found describing himself as "Chairmaker to His Majesty".

The tendency towards more disciplined and restrained design becomes increasingly evident towards the century's close. In the new type of walnut chair introduced from Holland soon after 1700 the form, purged of redundant ornament, was based upon the principle of contrasted curves. English makers were quick to appreciate the opportunity which this curvilinear principle afforded: the imported models were freely adapted and in the process largely transformed. When the type becomes fully naturalised, a continuous rhythm pervades the structure and the proportions are so nicely adjusted that even minor variations would falsify the scale. The finer specimens of these so-called "Queen Anne" chairs provide a remarkable instance of that newly awakened appreciation of form which manifests itself at this time throughout the whole decorative field. If the eighteenth century has strong claims to be regarded as the golden age of English craftsmanship, with the native tradition reinforced by the skilful assimilation of foreign techniques, we may well be disposed to hold that chair-makers at least never surpassed their achievements in the opening years.

At first slightly curved uprights enclose a wide splat pierced and carved with foliated ornament, while the front legs are of cabriole[9] form ending in hoof or club feet and united by stretchers. This form of leg, which had been gradually evolved, was the starting point of the whole development, the lines of the other members being made to conform. Later, the curve of the uprights becomes more pronounced; vase or fiddle splats follow the shape of the sitter's back; seat rails are rounded at the corners, and the legs, no longer united by stretchers, end in claw-and-ball feet—an Oriental motive of great antiquity now adopted as a favourite terminal. The splats, uprights and seat in chairs of high quality are veneered with figured burr walnut, while the more delicate carved ornament is applied (Fig. 53). Sometimes carving is replaced by marquetry decoration—the owner's crest amid mantling or a cypher and arabesques. Japanned chairs were produced in large numbers and often figure in contemporary inventories and notices of sales. Many were imported from trading stations in China, being made from European models and lacquered in the East; but time has taken a heavy toll of them, and few examples, imported or indigenous, now survive.

In upholstered chairs contemporary with the early curvilinear type, the cabriole form is adopted for the underframing, while for the coverings velvet, needlework, or tapestry was employed. Winged arm-chairs had been introduced toward the end of Charles II's reign, and the form soon became more or less standardised, the wings finishing in padded arm-rests with an outward curve. The Museum possesses a well-known example of these "Easie", or so-called "Grandfather" chairs, covered with the original needlework, which in this instance is of exceptional interest because the scenes are taken from plates in Ogilvy's folio *Virgil* published in 1658 (Fig. 48.)

About 1720 mahogany imported from the West Indies[9] began to be used for the manufacture of chairs on an extensive scale, gradually supplanting walnut as the fashionable wood.[10] The influence of this new material, hard and close-grained, and lending itself admirably to the purposes of the carver[11] is observable both in the design and decoration of chairs—the nature of the material always goes far to determine the design, to which ornament in its turn is inseparably related. With the introduction of mahogany there was a revulsion from dignified simplicity and a renewed demand for lavish enrichment. This change of taste, which declares itself unmistakably soon after the death of Queen Anne, inaugurates the second phase of the English baroque style, in which ornate splendour sometimes comes perilously near to vulgarity. Nothing is more characteristic than the ostentatious furniture decorated with animal and human motives which was fashionable early in George II's reign: essentially plastic in conception, it found an ideally suitable environment in the palatial Palladian houses of that magnificent age.

In the upholstered chairs with low backs and wide seats made to accommodate full-bottomed coats and crinolines the favourite lion motive was frequently employed: the head mask and paws, even the shaggy mane and hocks of the animal, constitute the salient ornament —realistically rendered and vigorously carved. Many of these chairs were gilded to match the monumental side-tables in saloons, and among the finest are those designed by William Kent for Sir Robert Walpole at Houghton Hall. The head and claws of an eagle were sometimes substituted as terminals (Fig. 59), and in the use of such motives (which have a pedigree dating back to the early French Renaissance) no consistency was attempted: while the arms end in lions' heads, a female mask may decorate the knees. This grandiose baroque type is not yet represented in the permanent collections, but in a set of twelve chairs and a table on loan from the Treasury the legs are vigorously modelled, the masks carved in high relief, and the mahogany has acquired the colour of bronze (Fig. 60).

Among the specialised varieties dating from the early years of the century are chairs made for reading or writing in a library. The occupant sat astride, resting his arms on the padded supports, with a book or writing material on the desk attached to the back. An example (Fig. 57) of these "library chairs" is of exceptional interest because originally it belonged to the poet, John Gay; while some manuscript verses in which this chair is described as "my throne unique" were found in a "secret" drawer below the seat.[12]

About 1740 the influence of the French *rocaille* style becomes discernible in the design and decoration of fashionable chairs, and baroque solidity is gradually superseded by lighter forms, rhythmical lines and delicate ornament in low relief. The solid splat is pierced and carved with scrolls and foliage: the line of the uprights becomes almost vertical, tapering upwards to meet the top rail which rises into a "cupid's bow" cresting; the seat rail is no longer rounded at the corners, and as an alternative to the cabriole, the straight leg united by stretchers is employed. In the following decade the rococo flood set in strongly,[13] fed by the tributary streams of the Gothic and Chinese. Though the craze for these pseudo-medieval and Oriental motives was a comparatively ephemeral vogue, it served to provide a wide repertory of ornament, which together with the makers' remarkable fertility of invention goes far to account for the extraordinary variety in the design of contemporary chairs. Another factor helps to explain this variety: patterns from now onward were widely disseminated through the publication of illustrated trade pattern-books. Of these, of course, Chippendale's *Director* (1st edition 1754) is by far the best known,[14] and in the ample selection of chairs there provided, free adaptations of French models are combined with "excursions into the Chinese and Gothic styles". Relatively few chairs in the mid-eighteenth century can be traced to any pattern book,[15] but the backs of a set (Fig. 70) in the Macquoid Bequest correspond with one of Chippendale's designs.[16] The fullest expression of rococo caprice is represented by chairs in which the splats are formed of interlaced ribbons realistically carved—a conceit which certainly violates functional propriety, however remarkable as a technical *tour de force*. Chippendale observes that "several sets have been made which have given entire satisfaction", and four chairs of very high quality from such a set are remarkably close to a plate in the *Director* (1st Edition, Pl. XVI) (Fig. 73). Here the legs end in scroll feet, a form of terminal borrowed from France and adapted as an alternative to the claw-and-ball.[17]

Grotesque travesties of Gothic ornament may be found in some contemporary patterns, and though Horace Walpole and a small circle of like-minded enthusiasts with a "relish" for the "true Gothic" affected to disdain such attempts of ignorant cabinet-makers, their own ventures of this kind were scarcely less absurd. The more extravagant flights of fancy were "unrealisable aspirations", and in general the characteristic motives were used only as a variant of the rococo, cusping and tracery being confined to the splat (Fig. 65). The Chinese "taste", on the other hand, has distinct claims to be regarded as an independent decorative convention—even perhaps as a definite style.

While the fashion for "Indian goods" of all kinds was, of course, of long standing, its inception dating back to the Elizabethan age, the late Stuart imitations were confined to surface decoration and, save in rare instances,[18] did not affect the structural form. With the revival of the taste just before the middle of the century there was an attempt to reproduce Oriental types—or rather to produce something that would pass as Chinese among those who had no first-hand acquaintance with the East. Sir William Chambers in his *Designs of Chinese Buildings, Furniture, etc.* (1757) gave two drawings from Chinese chairs,[19] but authentic models were not calculated to appeal to such fashionable designers as Chippendale, Darly and Halfpenny,[20] who for some years had been among the leading exponents of the vogue. It was far more consistently exploited than the Gothic for chairs. Backs and arms were filled with "Chinese railing": pagoda ornament being often introduced; seat rails were decorated with frets, and though the legs were generally quadrilateral, there are examples in which they are turned to imitate bamboo. Sometimes the Chinese motives were used merely as a flavouring and combined with rococo detail with charming effect: there may be a central splat formed of scrolls and foliage, while the treatment of the legs and pierced stretchers is resolutely "Chinese". At this time it was usual for one or more rooms in large houses to be furnished throughout in this pseudo-Oriental taste: in such apartments all was made to conform to the prevailing vogue, and the chairs were japanned to harmonise with the rest of the contents. Chippendale observes of his designs for such chairs in the *Director* that they are "very proper for a Lady's Dressing-Room especially if it is hung with India paper".

Standing somewhat apart from the main evolution are the "Windsor chairs", the most conspicuous of rustic varieties, produced from the end of the seventeenth century onwards amid the beech-woods of the Chilterns with High Wycombe as the centre. The salient characteristics of this type are the bent-wood bars, forming arms, backs and stretchers, and the use of dowel joints at the points of junction. In some examples the top-rail is shaped and supported on spindles with or without a central splat which is often pierced with a star, the Prince of Wales's plume, or other ornament; but the hooped back is a more familiar form. The seat is nearly always of elm, the bent members of ash or yew, the turned legs and spindles normally of beech. Windsor chairs were not confined to cottages and farm-houses: painted green, red or yellow they were frequently used in tea-gardens, and places of public resort, and were even to be found in lavishly furnished houses. The influence of contemporary fashion can be traced in details of the design—for instance in the Gothic variety, which may be regarded as the aristocrats of the type (Fig. 79). Here, spindles are replaced by a series of splats pierced with cusped tracery and contained within a pointed arch, the front legs of cabriole shape replacing the ordinary turned supports. Windsor chairs have never been superseded, and in the manufacture traditional patterns are still retained.

Among other specialised varieties are chairs introduced early in the eighteenth century for halls and corridors (Fig. 110). In the 3rd edition of the *Director* (1762) Chippendale illustrates six designs, and states that "they may be made of mahogany or any other wood, and painted". Often the arms and crest of the owner were painted in the centre of the back. Arm-chairs of exceptional size were also made in successive styles for the Masters of City Companies and Presidents of Freemasons' Lodges, the arms of the Company, or some symbolic device, figuring in many instances in the decoration.

Soon after the accession of George III a new and powerful impetus transformed the character of fashionable furniture. The 3rd edition of Chippendale's *Director* (1762) is devoted entirely to the rococo and its derivatives, but the period of indulgence in caprice and fancy was rapidly approaching its end. Robert Adam, after a long study of classic design and ornament in Italy and Dalmatia, had returned home and already become prominent as an architect. In 1761 he had

13

drawn out plans for providing the Duke of Northumberland with a suite of rooms at Syon which was to be "entirely in the Antique Style"—a date which may be taken to inaugurate the classical revival. Soon furniture and the whole range of domestic equipment manifested "the electric power of this revolution in art", though the transformation was not suddenly effected, and the introduction of classical motives in the decoration preceded any far-reaching structural change. An important example of this transitional phase is a gilt arm-chair (Fig. 81), one of a set formerly at 19 Arlington Street, which was designed by Adam in 1764 and probably made by Samuel Norman, a leading cabinet-maker, who supplied Sir Laurence Dundas with furniture "to the amount of ten thousand". It retains the curvilinear form of "French" rococo chairs but is carved with sphinxes and other classical motives. After the style had become fully established, Adam's ceremonial chairs for drawing-rooms and saloons corresponded closely with French models, though the ornament is generally larger in scale.[21] They were made of beech, or another soft wood, with the framework moulded and entirely gilt. The legs are tapered, or turned and fluted, and curved supports spring from cappings at the corners of the seat-rail to meet the bowed arms. Fine examples of these ceremonial chairs may still be seen at Osterley, and other great houses for which Adam was responsible.

The mahogany chairs of the classic revival afford a marked contrast to those in the rococo style. Once again, as in the early years of the century, the architect intervened (and on a more comprehensive scale) to determine the forms of furniture which were to accord with his decorative schemes. Symmetrical curves and studied proportions were now preferred to florid enrichment, and the carved or inlaid ornament drawn from the classical repertory of motives—husks, honeysuckle, wheat-ears, paterae and urns—was employed with an admirable sense of fitness and carefully related to the structural lines. The extent of the transformation can readily be appreciated if specimens of rococo and neo-classic chairs are compared (Figs. 74 & 90): it will be seen that they represent fundamentally different and conflicting ideals.

Horace Walpole, visiting Osterley in 1773, notes[22] that "the chairs are taken from antique lyres and make a charming harmony". Three large sets show with what resource a first-rate designer could adapt and vary this familiar classical form (Figs. 87–89). These chairs are veritable masterpieces of craftsmanship and in the pristine state in which they were delivered to the house. Another arm-chair (Fig. 92) is from a set in a room at Osterley decorated and furnished in the 'Etruscan' taste, and corresponds closely with a drawing in the Soane Museum dated 6 March 1776. Adam observes in the *Works in Architecture* that "a mode of decoration has been here attempted

14

which differs from any hitherto practiced in Europe". He confesses that ancient and modern authorities have failed to yield him any information concerning the interior decoration of the Etruscans, and explains that "the style of the ornament and colouring" are imitated from vases and urns. He enriched the low-toned palette of terracottas, yellows and browns with a judicious admixture of lighter hues. Delicate, slightly bizarre and small in scale, suited only to relatively confined spaces, Etruscan painting on walls and furniture never obtained an extensive vogue. In these Osterley chairs and in other fine examples of the style in its early phase, the backs are hooped or rectilinear; but oval, heart and shield-shaped backs soon became fashionable, slender curved ribs carved with paterae or festoons of drapery sometimes replacing the central splat (Figs. 96–97).

In trade publications of this period the style is seen translated into vernacular terms, purged of much of the classical character that fitted it for "the parade of life" and skilfully adapted to domestic use. A wide selection of patterns is represented, yet they do not amount to a tithe of the variety found in the contemporary chairs that still survive; for the classic formula in the later phases of the style was so freely interpreted that it imposed no severe restraint on the designer's fancy. The terms "Hepplewhite" and "Sheraton" are to be understood in a generic sense: many of the finest examples of the period bear no more than a general resemblance to illustrations in their books; none can be assigned to them on documentary grounds. Heart and shield shapes are particularly associated with Hepplewhite and Fig. 98 shows a chair which corresponds closely with a design in the *Guide* 1st edition (Pl. 4.); but he was certainly not responsible for introducing these shapes.

His avowed aim was "to exhibit the present taste" omitting such articles as were "the production of whim at the instance of caprice". In the first edition (1788) cabriole legs of attenuated form are still retained for "chairs of state" (*Guide*, Pl. 13, and cf. Fig. 94), and the scrolled "French foot" (favoured by Chippendale in the *Director*) is recommended as a terminal for seats of this kind. Hepplewhite draws attention to the concave shaping of the back, "the bars and frame sunk in a hollow, or rising in a round projection with a band or list on the inner and outer edges"—technical refinements which may be seen on many contemporary examples. In the Preface he observes that "a new and very elegant fashion has arisen within these few years" of finishing chairs with japanned decoration: this treatment allowed of a variety of grounds, so that seat furniture thus treated could be made to harmonise with the general colour-scheme of the room; while it had the further advantage that the framework might be "less massy than is requisite for mahogany". For decoration, floral garlands, sprays and medallions, painted in natural colours or grisaille, were employed. Hepplewhite's claim to have introduced the three feathers as an ornament is not established, for as the badge of the Prince of Wales's party it was in great request at the time. He illustrates an upholstered chair thus ornamented and with arms set "much higher than usual" which he says "has been executed with good effect for the Prince"—not necessarily by Hepplewhite's firm.

Explicit directions are given on the subject of upholstery. For japanned chairs with caned bottoms, cushions covered with linen are favoured to accord with the general hue: the strong and serviceable chairs made for dining-rooms should have "seats of horse hair, plain, striped or chequered etc., at pleasure"; while for upholstered chairs with square backs (shown in the third edition, 1794) seats of red or blue morocco leather tied down with silk tassels are recommended. In this "more elegant kind" medallions of printed or painted silk are to be inserted in the middle of the top rail, and the designs have a trivial, effeminate prettiness which seems like a distant foreshadowing of Victorian taste.

Though Sheraton admits that he went the round of the shops and the selection of chairs in the *Drawing Book* (published in parts 1791-4) may be in a measure derived from the fashionable models in use, he had greater fertility of invention than Hepplewhite; and late eighteenth-century pseudo-classicism—now tending to an extreme of feminine elegance—is seen at its best in the designs for chairs, as for other varieties of furniture in his book. The majority of the backs are rectilinear; and the central splat, which retains scarcely a trace of true classic feeling, is flanked in some instances by carved and moulded bars. These patterns for "Parlour chairs" convey a suggestion of perilous fragility—combined in the best examples with impeccable craftsmanship and a most discriminating selection of woods. Three designs are given for upholstered chairs to be used in drawing-rooms, which are to be "finished in white and gold, or the ornaments may be japanned". The tablets in the centre of the deep-shaped seat rail are "on French silk or satin, sewn on to the stuffing with borders round them", and seats and backs are to be decorated in the same style. Sheraton observes that "chairs of this kind have an effect which far exceeds any conception we can have of them from an uncoloured engraving or even of a coloured one"; but examples made from these patterns and still retaining their original upholstery do not appear to survive. Chintz "which may now be had of various patterns on purpose for chair seats", is also recommended for the drawing-room variety. Some designs are specially indicated as "suitable for japanning", and the explanatory notes show that the most fanciful models were intended for this treatment; they could also be made in mahogany, and directions are given by which their ornate character might be suitably "retrenched". Few chairs of this time were made of satinwood, probably because for seat furniture it was thought to be too aggressive in tone, but Fig. 105, one of these comparatively rare examples, is of exceptional interest because it corresponds with the arm-chairs in a large set made by the firm of Seddon for Hauteville House, Guernsey, in 1790. "Chair-making", writes Sheraton in his *Cabinet Dictionary* (1803) "is a branch generally confined to itself; as those who professedly work at it seldom make cabinet furniture". He adds that "the difference is remarkable in some chairs of precisely the same pattern when executed by different chair-makers, arising chiefly from the want of taste concerning the beauty of an outline, of which we judge by the eye more than the rigid rules of perspective". In this judging by the eye—an incommunicable faculty which defies analysis—lies the secret of the singular excellence of line and proportion that distinguishes so many late eighteenth-century chairs.

The Regency Style—miscalled, since George, Prince of Wales became Regent in 1811, and the term in this context is commonly understood to cover the period 1800–1820—was highly eclectic in character, "a medley or hotch-potch of all styles". The Roman, the Greek, the Egyptian, the Gothic, the Chinese, even the Etruscan and the Moresque, each contributed their quota to the mixture; though several of these were minor fashions, tributaries of the main stream, and by the straiter sect "Grecian severity" was consistently advocated as the ideal. This was "a more intense and archaeological" classic revival, drawing its inspiration from a variety of sources in the ancient world. At the outset it owed something to the French *Directoire* style as interpreted by Henry Holland, and, had he lived, the English version of Empire might have been closer to its proto-type; for he was a designer of genius with Gallican enthusiasms. But Holland died in 1806 when the "Regency" was still in the initial stage, and his brilliant gifts as a decorative artist (of which Southhill in Bedfordshire and the salvage from Carlton House at Buckingham Palace constitute the most impressive reminders) exercised little influence on the later phase. In its maturity Regency was a style in which "breadth and repose of surface, distinctness and contrast of outline and the opposition of plain and enriched parts"[23]—in short, a reliance on formal excellence, simplicity, solidity and sound use of material constitute the strongest appeal. Chairs are not among the varieties of furniture in which these qualities are most prominently displayed. None the less a resolute attempt was made by the more erudite designers to insure that they should conform to the new standards of orthodoxy: they were to reproduce as closely as possible the classic originals drawn by the protagonists of the movement on their travels abroad from bas-reliefs, vase-paintings and excavated remains. This aspiration was imperfectly realised. Thomas Hope, the most learned of the group, might write (in 1807) that the "pure taste of the antique reproduction of Greek forms for chairs, etc." had been restored; but he was powerless to restrain the later makers of trade-catalogues in whose publications the classic originals were not only adapted to contemporary domestic use—"taking not so much the mere pattern or imitation, but the spirit and principle on which the original was composed",[24] but in some instances outrageously travestied as well.

By the votaries of the new cult of antiquity the models for chairs provided by the earlier neo-classical revival were regarded as hopelessly obsolete, and soon far-reaching changes affected the form. There is a marked emphasis on horizontal lines, and prominent features are the curved or "sabre"-shaped front legs, the arms set high on the back uprights giving "a characteristic high-shouldered appearance"; the top rail swept backwards and forming a continuous curve with the rear legs. "Parlour chairs" were made of mahogany or rosewood inlaid with foliated patterns and stringing lines of brass (Fig. 120): many were japanned (for the fashion still persisted), classical motives in the decoration tending to supplant the naturalistic detail hitherto in vogue. In the more ambitious specimens the archaeological bias of the movement is plainly declared. Thomas Hope recommends antique heads of "helmeted warriors, winged figures emblematical of freedom, and lances surmounted by a Phrygian Cap of Liberty" as suitable ornaments for chairs; while archaic lions, gryphons, sphinxes, owls and winged female terminals (Fig. 116) were also included in what, with the increasing mania for symbolism,[25] became a veritable menagerie of animal forms. The armchair (Fig. 114) is of exceptional interest because it closely corresponds with a design dated 1804 and published by George Smith in his *Household Furniture* (Plate 56). The types for dining-room and parlour tended towards standardisation, and it was into the arms and legs of drawing-room chairs that these "heads of various animals" were introduced—a practice sanctioned by French precedent for which in the later phases of the movement an almost superstitious reverence was shown. Other Regency varieties—bergère, "conversation" and "hunting chairs" are not yet represented in the Museum collections.

Sheraton in his *Encyclopaedia* (1807) observes that in chair-making "it is extremely difficult to attain to anything really novel", and recommends those who are avid for novelties to sit down and see what they can do in that way themselves. This complaint, a confession of bankrupt invention, is echoed by later designers, and in pattern books published in the twenties there is a reversion to earlier forms, suggesting that many extant examples are often dated some years before they were made. The Regency style proved to be endowed with surprising vitality, and, despite increasing signs of decadence in design preluding the Victorian debacle, lingered on until the end of George IV's reign.

REFERENCES AND NOTES

(1) In the Royal Writs issued under Henry III ordering furniture for the King's private apartments, chairs are among the objects specified: a movable chair (cathedra mobilis) is mentioned.

(2) Though in the capital and a few provincial cities, such as Chester and York, guild regulations were rigidly enforced, they did not apply in country districts. Under James I the Shuttleworths of Gawthorpe employed a "dish-thrower" to make them a "thrown chair". (Shuttleworth Accounts. Chetham Society. Vol. 35, p. 160.)

(3) Now exhibited in Room I.

(4) For evidence that chairs of this type were made for the Crown by Coffermakers and that their production was a specialised craft, see R. W. Symonds "The Craft of the Coffermaker", *Connoisseur*, March 1941.

(5) In Elizabethan inventories of great houses, upholstered chairs, apparently made in sets, are listed and are sometimes described as covered "suteable" (or to match) a bed.

(6) A French engraver, 1602–76.

(7) *Sylva* (1st edition, 1664).

(8) The term is now used to denote "a form of leg which curves outward . . . and then descends in a tapering reverse curve terminating in an ornamental foot" (Webster). In this sense it has no contemporary authority. In Hepplewhite's *Guide* (1788) it is used to describe a variety of chair with a "stuffed" back.

(9) Early importations of so-called "Spanish mahogany" were obtained mainly from the West Indies, notably from Jamaica and Cuba and the Spanish Mainland; while the later and inferior variety came from Honduras in Central America.

(10) Many fine walnut chairs were, however, made down to the middle of the 18th century.

(11) The surfaces of chairs were no longer veneered.

(12) They are included in an edition of Gay's *Poems* published in 1820, in which an engraving of the chair forms the frontispiece.

(13) But the rococo was never exploited "in the most advanced degree" on chairs, as for example on contemporary picture frames.

(14) Darly's *New Book of Chinese, Gothic and Modern Chairs* (1752) is the only considerable work published before the *Director* which aimed at providing assistance to the trade.

(15) The most important in this connection are Ince and Mayhew's *Universal System of Household Furniture* (1759–63), where some of the designs are obvious plagiarisms from *Director* plates, Manwaring's *The Cabinet and Chair Makers' Real Friend and Companion* (1765) and *The Chair Makers' Guide* (1766)—the last two intended for those who specialised in chairs.

(16) *Director*, 1st Edition Pl. XII. Though there is a strong probability that these and certain other chairs, which closely follow a design in the *Director*, were made by Chippendale's firm, only a bill could afford positive proof. Another set (Tomes Bequest) have straight legs and the same backs slightly simplified.

(17) In the *Director* there is only one design showing the claw-and-ball (3rd Edition, Pl. XVIII, right).

(18) E.g. the japanned chairs in the Blue Drawing-Room at Ham, Fig. 44.

(19) He notes that they are among the "movables of the saloon" and are "made sometimes of rosewood, ebony or lacquered work, and sometimes of bamboo".

(20) William Halfpenny's *New Designs for Chinese Buildings*, 1750, in which a few designs for chairs are given, is the earliest publication of the kind, but the author states that the "Chinese manner" had been "already introduced here with success".

(21) But the classical revival in England ante-dates that in France, and a searching investigation of the chronology would be necessary before it could be safely asserted that Adam was indebted to the French. As coverings, figured damask and tapestry were employed.

(22) In a letter to the Countess of Upper Ossory, 21 June 1773.

(23) Hope, *Household Furniture* (1807), p. 2.

(24) George Smith, *Household Furniture* (1808). Preface p. vi.

(25) This aspect of the style is extremely prominent in the later trade catalogues, e.g. Richard Brown's *Rudiments of Drawing Cabinet and Upholstery Furniture* (1822). Though Brown is perhaps the worst offender in the matter of symbolism, he rebukes makers who "for the sake of notoriety" talk of Trafalgar Chairs and Waterloo feet.

LIST OF ILLUSTRATIONS

13. ARM-CHAIR AND FOOTSTOOL. Beechwood upholstered in velvet originally crimson, trimmed with galon and fringed, and studded with brass-headed nails. Formerly in possession of William Juxon (d. 1663), Archbishop of Canterbury, at Little Compton Manor House, near Moreton-in-Marsh, Gloucestershire. The fact that Juxon attended Charles I on the scaffold gave rise to the long-standing but probably erroneous belief that it is the chair in which Charles I sat at his trial in Westminster Hall. Early 17th century. H. 4 ft. 2 in., W. 2 ft. 9 in. Footstool. H. 1 ft. 7¾ in., W. 1 ft. 9¾ in. *Bought with the aid of a grant from the National Art-Collections Fund.*

W.12–13–1928

14. CHAIR. ("Farthingale" type.) Oak, upholstered later in knotted woollen pile ("Turkey work"). Early 17th century. H. 3 ft. 1 in., W. 1 ft. 7 in. *Bequeathed by Col. G. B. Croft Lyons.* W.63–1926

15. CHAIR. ("Farthingale" type.) Walnut, covered with figured blue cloth decorated with applied embroidery. Early 17th century. H. 3 ft., W. 1 ft. 10 in. W.1–1912

16. ARM-CHAIR. Walnut and beechwood covered with green velvet. The mahogany stretchers are eighteenth-century replacements. First half of the seventeenth century. H. 3 ft. 4 in., W. 2 ft. 4 in. *Given by the seventh Duke of Buccleuch.* W.31–1918

17. ARM-CHAIR. Oak. Back and seat covered with knotted woollen pile ("Turkey Work"). From Beau Desert, Warwickshire. Mid 17th century. H. 3 ft. 2 in., W. 2 ft. 4 in. W.30–1923

18. CHAIR. Turned walnut upholstered in tent-stitch embroidery. The arms of Hill of Spaxton Yarde and Pounsford, co. Somerset, impaling Gurdon of Assington Hall, co. Suffolk, and Letton, co. Norfolk, relate to the marriage in 1641 of Roger Hill of Pounsford (d. 29th June 1655) with his second wife Abigail (d. 3rd December 1658), born Gurdon. From Denham Place, Bucks. Between 1641–1655. H 3 ft. 1 in., W. 1 ft. 8½ in. W.124–1937

19. ARM-CHAIR. Oak, the back panel carved with a vase and conventional foliage. Lancashire type. About 1640–50. H. 3 ft. 8 in., W. 2 ft. W.33–1938

20. CHAIR. Carved and turned oak. Lancashire type. Dated 1641. H. 3 ft. 10 in., W. 1 ft. 10 in. W.10–1947

21. CHAIR. Turned and carved oak. Yorkshire or Derbyshire; mid 17th century. H. 3 ft. 2½ in., W. 1 ft. 7 in. 86–1893

22. CHAIR. Oak, carved and turned. Yorkshire or Derbyshire; mid 17th century. H. 3 ft. 4¾ in., W. 1 ft. 6½ in. 84–1893

23. CHAIR. Oak covered with leather studded with brass-headed nails. The front legs and stretcher of knob turning. About 1650. H. 2 ft. 11 in., W. 1 ft. 7 in. W.9–1923

24. CHAIR. Oak covered with leather studded with brass-headed nails. The carved stretcher resembles those on early Post-Restoration walnut chairs. About 1660. H. 3 ft. 2¾ in., W. 1 ft. 6½ in. 94–1893

25. CHILD'S ARM-CHAIR. Carved and turned oak inlaid with holly and bog oak. Carved (behind the top-rail) with initials RW and date 1680. But the chair probably dates from about 1625. H. 3 ft. 10 in., W. 1 ft. 6½ in.   W.6–1946

26. CHILD'S CHAIR. Oak turned and carved in relief. Mid 17th century. H. 3 ft. 4½ in., W. 1 ft. 7½ in.   397–1890

27. CHILD'S CHAIR. Turned walnut. About 1660–70. H. 2 ft. 10 in., W. 1 ft. 7½ in.   W.31–1913

28. CHILD'S CHAIR. Carved and turned walnut, with caned seat and back. About 1685. H. 3 ft. 9¾ in., W. 1 ft. 4½ in.   W.89–1910

29. CHAIR-TABLE. Carved oak with applied ornament. The back, revolving on pins, tips forward to form a table. About 1650–60. H. 4 ft. 5 in., W. 2 ft. 2 in.   W.45–1948

30. ARM-CHAIR. Walnut spirally turned; caned back and seat. About 1665. H. 3 ft. 5 in., W. 2 ft. 2 in.   W.64–1911

31. CHAIR. Carved and turned walnut with cane seat and back. About 1675. H. 3 ft. 11½ in., W. 2 ft. *One of a set given by Mr. Leslie Clarke.*
                                                                  W.39–1940

32. CHAIR. Carved and turned walnut, caned back and seat. About 1670–5. H. 3 ft. 11 in., W. 1 ft. 8 in.   W.61–1925

33. ARM-CHAIR. Carved and turned walnut with cane back and seat. About 1675. H. 4 ft. 3 in., W. 2 ft. *Given by Sir George Donaldson.* W.145–1919

34. CHAIR. Beechwood, carved and painted black, with seat upholstered in *tent-stitch* embroidery. H. 4 ft. 4½ in., W. 1 ft. 8⅛ in. About 1690. *Given by Mr. Frank Green.*   W.37–1916

35. CHAIR. Carved walnut. Cane back; seat upholstered in green velvet. About 1690. From the Mulliner Collection. H. 4 ft. 7 in., W. 1 ft. 6 in. *Given by Mr. R. Freeman Smith*   W 31–1925

36. CHAIR. Carved and painted beech wood. About 1690–5. H. 4 ft. 3½ in., W. 1 ft. 6½ in.   W.71–1911

37. CHAIR. Carved and turned walnut with oval back and circular seat covered with leather, fixed with brass nails. From Boughton House, Northamptonshire. 1675–80. H. 3 ft. 4 in., W. 1 ft. 6 in. *Given by the seventh Duke of Buccleuch.*   W.34–1918

38. ARM-CHAIR. Carved walnut, upholstered in black leather, with an iron ratchet for adjusting the back. About 1680. H. 3 ft. 11¾ in., W. 2 ft. 3 in.   W.40–1927

39. "SLEEPING CHAIR". Carved and gilt with adjustable back. Covered with the original crimson brocade matching the wall hangings. One of a pair at Ham House Petersham. Described in an inventory made for the Duke of Lauderdale in 1679 (the approximate date of the chairs). H. 4 ft. 3½ in., W. 2 ft. 5½ in.

40. ARM-CHAIR. Carved with dolphin motives, painted and gilt. Covered with the original crimson brocaded satin. At Ham House, Petersham. One of a set of twelve described in an inventory dated 1679 (the approximate date of the set). H. 3 ft. 3½ in., W. 2 ft. 1 in.

41. ARM-CHAIR. Walnut, turned and carved, with gilt enrichments. Covered with original figured velvet. At Ham House, Petersham. About 1675. H. 3 ft. 8½ in., W. 2 ft. 1 in.

42. ARM-CHAIR. Beechwood painted black and parcel gilt. Covered with original yellow satin decorated with red cord appliqué, a rare form of late 17th-century upholstery. One of a set at Ham House, Petersham. About 1685. H. 3 ft. 8½ in. W. 2 ft. 3½ in.

43. ARM-CHAIR. Carved and gilt wood, covered with green velvet. About 1680. H. 3 ft. 7 in., W. 2 ft. 2 in. *Given by the seventh Duke of Buccleuch.* W.32–1918

44. CHAIR. Wood, japanned in polychrome on a dark ground with oriental motives. The cresting bears the cipher and coronet of Elizabeth Dysart, Duchess of Lauderdale. One of a set at Ham House, Petersham, probably that described in an inventory dated 1683 as " 12 back stooles with cane bottoms, japanned ". An early and naïve attempt to imitate an Oriental form. About 1680. H. 4 ft. 2½ in., W. 1 ft. 8½ in.

45. CHAIR (one of three). Walnut upholstered in green velvet. About 1690. H. 3 ft. 1½ in., W. 1 ft. 9 in. *Given by Mr. Douglas Eyre, in memory of his father and mother.* W.27–1922

46. CHAIR. Carved walnut upholstered in red velvet. Style of Daniel Marot. A set of eighteen similar chairs at Hampton Court Palace were supplied by Richard Roberts, Chairmaker to George I, in 1717, and in the receipt are described as having " India backs ", presumably in reference to the pierced carving. H. 3 ft. 10 in., W. 1 ft. 9¾ in.
W.28–1909

47. CHAIR. Beechwood, japanned green and gold on a red ground. About 1710. H. 3 ft. 9 in., W. 1 ft. 10 in. W.44–1938

48. WING ARM-CHAIR. Walnut upholstered in embroidery of coloured wools (*tent and cross stitch*) with eleven scenes after illustrations engraved by Wenceslaus Hollar and Pierre Lombart after Franz Cleyn, for the folio *Virgil*, edited and printed by John Ogilby (1600–76), London, 1658. About 1700. H. 3 ft. 11 in., W. 2 ft. 8 in. *Given by Mr. Douglas Eyre in memory of his father and mother.* W.25–1922

49. CHAIR. Turned and painted beech upholstered in Soho tapestry. One of a pair. Early 18th century. H. 3 ft. 9 in., W. 1 ft. 11½ in. *Given by Mr. F. W. Green.* W.8–1932

50. CHAIR. Walnut upholstered in *tent-stitch* embroidery. About 1715. H. 3 ft. 3¼ in., W. 1 ft. 10¼ in. Seat cover a restoration. *Given by Mr. Frank Green.* W.34–1916

51. CHAIR. Carved and gilt gesso, with upholstery in crimson and gold figured velvet. A similar velvet, ordered from John Johnson & Co., Mercers, in July 1714, covers Queen Anne's bed and the accompanying chairs and stools at Hampton Court Palace. About 1715. H. 3 ft. 3¾ in., W. 2 ft. 0½ in.   W.15–1931

52. CHAIR. Beechwood. Carved and gilt gesso. Upholstered in red and gold cut velvet of the early 18th century. Cresting carved with the arms (*sable three nags' heads erased argent*) granted in April 1717 to Sir William Humphreys, Bart, Lord Mayor of London 1714–15. About 1717. H. 4 ft. 0 in., W. 2 ft. 0½ in.   W.62–1935

53. CHAIR. Walnut, carved and in part veneered. One of a set. About 1715. H. 3 ft. 4 in., W. 1 ft. 11 in.   680–1890

54. CHAIR (one of a pair). Walnut carved and in part veneered. About 1720. H. 3 ft. 3½ in., W. 1 ft. 9¾ in.   W.26–1912

55. CHAIR. Walnut, carved and in part veneered. About 1720–5. H. 3 ft. 3 in., W. 1 ft. 9½ in. *One of a pair given by Sir Paul Makins, Bart.*   W.37–1920

56. ARM-CHAIR ("Writing-Chair"). Carved walnut, with seat upholstered in velvet. The arms terminate in eagles' heads. About 1720. H. 2 ft. 9 in., W. 2 ft. 1 in. *Given by Mrs. M. Marchant.*   W.42–1924

57. READING AND WRITING CHAIR. Carved mahogany upholstered in leather. Formerly in the possession of the poet John Gay (1685–1732). About 1720. H. 2 ft. 9 in., W. 2 ft. 7 in.   W.47–1948
Such chairs were used in libraries. Sheraton in his *Cabinet Dictionary* (1803) illustrates a late variety and writes ". . . the reader places himself with his back to the front of the chair, and rests his arms on the top yoke".

58. CHAIR. Walnut. The back and seat covered with blue leather, parcel gilt and embossed. About 1720. H. 3 ft. 6 in., W. 1 ft. 11½ in.   235–1898

59. ARM-CHAIR. Carved walnut upholstered in red velvet. About 1725. H. 3 ft. 6 in., W. 2 ft. 8¾ in. *Given by the children of the late Sir George Donaldson in his memory.*   W.38–1925
Eagles' heads and claws were sometimes adopted as terminals as an alternative to the favourite lion motives of the early Georgian period.

60. CHAIR. Carved mahogany, covered with original green leather. One of a set of furniture made for the Treasury. About 1730. *Lent by the Treasury.*

61. CHAIR. Carved and gilt wood, one of a set at Ham House, Petersham. About 1725–30. The underframing represents a revival of the X form, which dates back to the Middle Ages.

62. CHAIR. Walnut, upholstered in *tent-* and *cross-stitch* needlework. Mid 18th century. H. 3 ft. 3 in., W. 1 ft. 7 in. *One of a set of six bequeathed by Lady W. S. Theobald.*   W.19–1938

63. CHAIR. Carved mahogany. One of a set. About 1740. In the centre of the splat the crest of Eyre. H. 3 ft. 2½ in., W. 2 ft. *Given by Mr. Douglas Eyre.*   W.32–1922

64. PRESIDENT'S CHAIR. Carved mahogany with painted and gilt detail. Made for the President of Lyon's Inn, an Inn of Chancery, Newcastle Street, Strand. About 1750. H. 4 ft. 2 in., W. 2 ft. 9¼ in. W.63–1911

   Large presidential chairs elaborately carved were made at this period for the City Companies, Masonic Lodges and the Inns of Court.

65. CHAIR. Mahogany. The back carved in "Gothic" taste. About 1760–5. H. 3 ft. 2 in., W. 1 ft. 10 in. *Given by Mr. Eric Browett in memory of his wife.* W.65–1937

66. ARM-CHAIR. Carved mahogany, the seat upholstered in contemporary needlework. About 1760. H. 3 ft. 4½ in., W. 2 ft. 6½ in. *One of a pair bequeathed by Lady W. S. Theobald.* W.12–1938

   The pillar form of the front legs resembles that shown in a design for "Gothic chairs" in Chippendale's *Director*, Plate 25, 3rd Edit. (1762).

67. CHAIR. Carved mahogany. One of a pair. About 1760. H. 3 ft. 1½ in., W. 1 ft. 11½ in. *Croft Lyons Bequest.* W.56–1926

68. CHAIR. Carved mahogany. About 1760. H. 3 ft. 1¾ in. W. 2 ft. 10 in. *One of a set of six given by Mrs. Viva Jeyes.* W.116–1937

69. CHAIR. Carved mahogany. One of a set of six. Backs corresponding with *Director*, 3rd Edition, 1762, plate XIII (dated 1753) No. 3. Mid 18th century. H. 3 ft. 1 in., W. 1 ft. 11 in. About 1755. *Tomes Bequest.* W.62–1940

   The "shoe" or moulded base beneath one of the splats is inscribed in pencil "*6 pedestals for Mr. Chippendale's backs*". This implies either that the "backs" were obtained ready-made from Chippendale, or that they were copied from his designs.

70. ARM-CHAIR. Carved mahogany, the seat upholstered in needlework of coloured silks and wools. Closely similar to a design dated 1753, Chippendale's *Director*, 1st Edition, 1754, plate XII (3) and probably made by his firm. (Cf. No 71.) H. 3 ft. 1¾ in., W. 2 ft. 2½ in. *Macquoid Bequest.* W.46–1925

71. Design for a chair from Thomas Chippendale's *Director*, 1st edition, 1754, plate XII. (Cf. No. 70.)

72. ARM-CHAIR. Carved mahogany. The splat resembles designs for "Ribband Back" chairs in Chippendale's *Director*, 1st Edition, 1754, plate XVI. About 1755. H. 4 ft. 4¾ in., W. 2 ft. 2¾ in. *Croft Lyons Bequest.* W.54–1926

73. CHAIR. Carved mahogany with seat upholstered in contemporary needlework. The splat resembles designs for "Ribband Back" chairs in Chippendale's *Director*, 1st edition, 1754, plate XVI. One of four. About 1755. H. 3 ft. 3½ in., W. 2 ft. 2 in. *Clarke Bequest.* W.65–1935.

74. ARM-CHAIR. Carved mahogany. Closely corresponds with a design, dated 1759, in Chippendale's *Director*, 3rd edition, plate XXII, one of the designs for "French Chairs" which does not occur in the 1st edition (1754). About 1760. (The damask modern.) H. 3 ft. 6½ in., W. 2 ft. 5 in. *Given by Brigadier W. E. Clark, C.M.G., D.S.O.* W.47–1946

75. CHAIR. Carved mahogany. Back filled with lattice-work, legs and stretchers decorated with frets; in the "Chinese" taste. (Cf. Chippendale's *Director*, 1754, plates XXIII–XXV.) About 1755–60. H. 3 ft. 4 in., W. 1 ft. 10½ in.   W.13–1911

76. ARM-CHAIR. Beech with parquetry of walnut and sycamore. Back and arms filled with lattice-work; inlaid with chequer and key patterns. About 1760–5. H. 2 ft. 7¾ in., W. 1 ft. 9⅜ in. *Given by Mr. Randolph Behrens.*   884–1901

77. CHAIR. Carved mahogany. One of a pair. About 1765. Bears some resemblance to the designs of Robert Manwaring, author of the *Cabinet and Chairmakers' Real Friend and Companion.* H. 3 ft. 3 in., W. 2 ft. *Given by Mr. Frank Green.*   W.9–1932

78. CHAIR. ("Windsor" type.) Wood painted black. Bequeathed by Oliver Goldsmith in 1774 to his friend William Hawes, M.D., founder of the Royal Humane Society. Mid 18th century. H. 3 ft. 1¾ in., W. 2 ft. 1 in. *Given by Lady Hawes, widow of Sir Benjamin Hawes* (b. 1797, d. 1862).   538–1872

79. ARM-CHAIR. Turned and carved yew. "Windsor" type, in the "Gothick" taste. Mid 18th century. H. 3 ft. 3½ in., W. 1 ft. 11 in. *Bequeathed by Mrs. S. I. Woodley.*   W.12–1940

80. ARM-CHAIR. Mahogany. About 1760–70. Formerly in the possession of the poet William Cowper (1731–1800). H. 3 ft. 6 in., W. 2 ft. 7 in. *Given by Mr. H. B. Tait.*   W.21–1933

81. ARM-CHAIR. Beechwood carved and gilt. Part of a set of four arm-chairs and settee made, probably, by Samuel Norman (*fl.* 1754–64), from designs by Robert Adam, dated 1764 (in the Soane Museum), for Sir Lawrence Dundas, Bt., of Moor Park, Hertfordshire. From No. 19 Arlington Street, his London residence. H. 3 ft. 6 in., W. 2 ft. 6½ in.   W.1–1937

82. ARM-CHAIR. Carved, gilt and upholstered with sprigged satin. The back supported by winged sphinxes. One of a set, designed by Robert Adam, in the state bedroom at Osterley. For the original drawing see No. 83. H. 3 ft. 3¾ in., W. 2 ft. 1 in.

83. Design for an arm-chair for the state bedroom at Osterley, by Robert Adam; dated 24 April 1777. The drawing is in the Soane Museum (*Adam*, vol. 17, No. 97). See No. 82.

84. ARM-CHAIR. Carved and gilt. One of a set in the Tapestry Room at Osterley. The tapestry covers woven by Neilson at the Gobelins factory in 1775, to match the wall-hangings. The chairs, probably designed by Adam, have close affinities with contemporary French models. H. 3 ft. 2 in., W. 2 ft. 1½ in.

85. ARM-CHAIR. Carved and gilt wood with upholstery in modern green damask. About 1775. H. 3 ft. 5 in., W. 2 ft. 1 in. *Given by the Ministry of Works.*   W.42–1946

86. PRESIDENT'S CHAIR. Carved and inlaid mahogany, upholstered in green leather. About 1770. H. 5 ft. 10 in., W. 2 ft. 3 in.

W.10–1923

87. CHAIR. Carved mahogany, with lyre-shaped splat. One of a set, designed by Robert Adam, in the eating room at Osterley Park. The original drawing is in the Soane Museum (*Adam*, vol. 17, No. 93). About 1775. H. 3 ft., W. 1 ft. 8½ in.

88. ARM-CHAIR. Carved mahogany, with splat composed of a lyre with patera and honeysuckle motives. One of a set, probably designed by Robert Adam, in the Breakfast Room at Osterley Park. About 1775. H. 2 ft. 11 in., W. 2 ft. 0¼ in.

89. ARM-CHAIR, the frame veneered with rosewood; inlaid decoration and splat of satinwood; the legs headed with swags of ormolu. One of a set, probably designed by Adam, in the Library at Osterley Park. About 1775. H. 2 ft. 11 in., W. 2 ft. 0¾ in.

90. ARM-CHAIR. Carved mahogany. Splat lyre-shaped with metal strings. Style of Robert Adam. About 1775. H. 2 ft. 10½ in., W. 1 ft. 11 in.

45–1869

91. ARM-CHAIR. Beechwood, painted to represent satinwood and decorated with neo-classical motives. One of a set at Osterley Park. About 1775. H. 3 ft., W. 2 ft.

92. ARM-CHAIR. Painted beechwood with caned seat. One of a set, designed by Robert Adam, in the Etruscan Room at Osterley Park. The original drawing, dated 25 January 1776, is in the Soane Museum (*Adam*, vol. 17, No. 96). H. 2 ft. 11¾ in., W. 2 ft. 2¼ in.

93. ARM-CHAIR. Mahogany. The splat pierced and carved with a vase and honeysuckle ornament. About 1770.

503–1907

94. CHAIR. Carved mahogany, with "Ladder-back", about 1775. This type of back was first introduced in the late Stuart period and revived in the middle of the eighteenth century. The legs represent the last phase of the cabriole as shown in Hepplewhite's *Guide* (1788). H. 3 ft. 1½ in., W. 2 ft. 0½ in. *Given by Mr. Eric M. Browett in memory of his wife.*

W.72–1937

95. ARM-CHAIR. Carved mahogany; back with "Gothic" arcading. About 1775. H. 3 ft. W. 2 ft. 1 in. *Given by Mr. Edward Dent.* W.21–1922

96. ARM-CHAIR. Carved mahogany, with Prince of Wales's feathers. About 1775. The motive of the Prince of Wales's feathers is found in Hepplewhite's *Guide*, 1st edition, 1788, plate 8. (Cf. also, Nos. 102 and 104.) H. 3 ft. 2½ in., W. 2 ft.

1458–1904

97. ARM-CHAIR. Carved mahogany. One of a set of nine acquired by Jonathan Pytts for his house, Kyre Park, Worcestershire, 1776–81. About 1775. H. 3 ft. 3 in., W. 1 ft. 10½ in.

W.2–1946

98. CHAIR. Mahogany, inlaid with boxwood paterae. The splat closely resembles a design in Hepplewhite's *Guide*, 1st edition, 1788, plate 4. H. 3 ft., W. 1 ft. 8 in. *Given by Mrs. A. R. Hatley.*

W.19–1934

99. CHAIR. Carved mahogany. The turned and fluted legs headed with lotus cappings. About 1785. H. 3 ft. 1 in., W. 1 ft. 10 in.   W.68–1935

100. CHAIR. Mahogany, carved with classical ornament and inset with a panel of painted satinwood. About 1785. H. 3ft. 1½ in., W. 1 ft. 8 in.
510–1907

101. CHAIR. Carved mahogany. Maker's or owner's name in ink under the seat frame: *Samuel Fairhead August 1783.* H. 2 ft. 10¾ in., W. 1 ft. 9 in.   W.71–1940

102. CHAIR. Carved mahogany. The back based on a plate (No. 28) in Sheraton's Drawing Book (1791–94). H. 2 ft. 11 in., W. 1 ft. 9 in. *Given by Mr. Eric Browett in memory of his wife.*   W.70–1937

103. ARM-CHAIR. Mahogany painted black and ivory with decorative detail in colour. About 1780–85. H. 3 ft. 1¼ in., D. 1 ft. 10 in.
W.52–1946

104. ARM-CHAIR. Beechwood, painted or "japanned" in colours. Splat in the form of Prince of Wales's feathers. About 1790. H. 3 ft. 1½ in., W. 1 ft. 10 in. (Cf. No. 96.)   W.90–1911

105. ARM-CHAIR. Satinwood painted in colours. This arm-chair corresponds exactly in design and decoration with a set of painted satinwood supplied by Seddon, Sons and Shackleton to D. Tupper, of Guernsey, about 1790. H. 3 ft. 0½ in., W. 1 ft. 8⅞ in. *Given by Mrs. Simon Green.*   W.59–1936

106. ARM-CHAIR. Beechwood with decoration painted or "japanned" in polychrome. One of four. About 1795. H. 3 ft. 0¾ in., W. 1 ft. 9¾ in. *Given by Mr. Richard Crossley Sharman.*   W.3–1941

107. ARM-CHAIR. Turned beech with decoration "japanned" in black and gold. About 1800. H. 2 ft. 9¼ in., W. 1 ft. 10⅛ in.   999–1897

108. ARM-CHAIR. Beechwood, "japanned" in black and gold. In the centre of the caned oval a medallion of papier mâché painted in grisaille. About 1800. H. 2 ft. 9 in., W. 1 ft. 9 in.   332–1899

109. ARM-CHAIR. Painted beechwood; the slats decorated with wheat-ear motives. At Osterley Park. About 1790. H. 3 ft. 11 in., W. 2 ft.

110. HALL-CHAIR. Painted beechwood. One of a pair. From David Garrick's Villa at Hampton, Middlesex. About 1775. Chippendale's firm furnished Garrick's house in the Adelphi; the Museum possesses the bills dated 1771–72. It may be assumed that the villa at Hampton was furnished from the same source. H. 3 ft. 2½ in., W. 1 ft. 9 in.
W.32–1937

111. HALL CHAIR. Mahogany, carved with classical ornament. About 1800. H. 2 ft. 7 in., W. 1 ft. 2 in.   784–1896

112. CHAIR. Marquetry of various woods with brass stringing lines. About 1795–1800. H. 3 ft., W. 1 ft. 6½ in.   407–1872

113. ARM-CHAIR. Beechwood, "japanned" black with brass mounts. About 1810. H. 2 ft. 8 in., W. 1 ft. 10 in.   W.30–1935

114. ARM-CHAIR. Wood carved in relief and painted black, with gilt detail. In the "Egyptian" taste. About 1810. Based on a design in Smith's *Household Furniture*, 1808, plate 56. (Cf. No. 115.) H. 3 ft., W. 2 ft. 1¾ in. *Bequeathed by Mr. Edward Knoblock.* W.14–1945

115. Design for an arm-chair from George Smith's *Household Furniture*, 1808, plate 56. (Cf. No. 114.)

116. ARM-CHAIR. Beechwood, carved, gilt, and "japanned" dark green. Female terminal figures in the "Grecian" taste. About 1810. H. 2 ft. 10½ in., W. 2 ft. W.5–1939

117. ARM-CHAIR. Stained and varnished beechwood with caned seat and back. About 1810. H. 2 ft. 10 in., W. 1 ft. 10 in. W.11–1931

118. ARM-CHAIR. Grained and gilt with upholstered seat and back. One of a pair. Based on a design by Thomas Hope in *Household Furniture*, 1807, plate 22. H. 3 ft. 6 in., W. 2 ft. 3 in. W49.–1949

119. ARM-CHAIR. Mahogany inlaid with brass. About 1810–15. H. 2 ft. 10 in., W. 1 ft. 9¾ in. *Given by Lieut.-Colonel R. Leslie.*
W.4–1938

120. CHAIR. Beechwood and mahogany with brass inlay. About 1820. H. 2 ft. 9 in., W. 1 ft. 6 in. W.10–1909

ILLUSTRATIONS

1. From a French illumination. *About* 1400.

2. Box-Chair. Carved oak. *About* 1525.

3. Arm-Chair, caquetoire type. Carved oak. *About* 1540.

4. Box-Chair. Carved oak. *Dated* 1574.

5. Arm-Chair, caquetoire type. Carved oak. *Late* 16th century.

6. Carved oak. *Early* 17th century.

7. Carved and painted oak. *About* 1600.

8. Carved and inlaid oak. *About* 1600.

9. Carved and turned oak. *Dated* 1682.

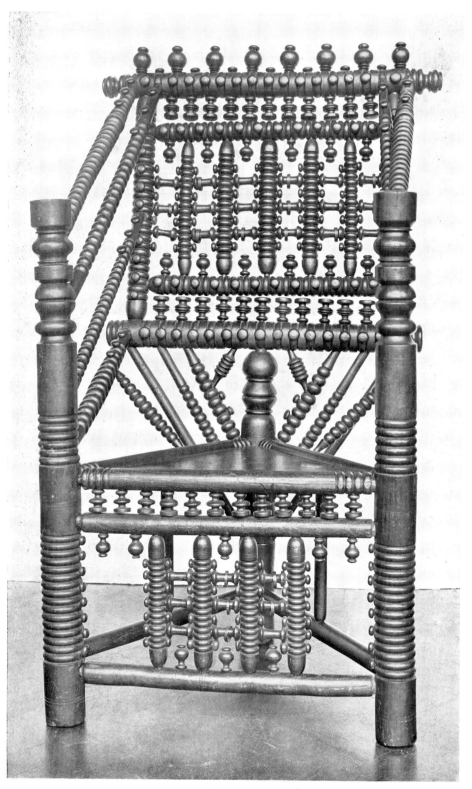

10. Turned ash and oak. *Early* 17th century.

11. Turned oak. *1st half* of the 17th century.

12. Turned and carved oak. *Late* 16th *or early* 17th century.

13. Upholstered and covered in velvet. *Early* 17th century.

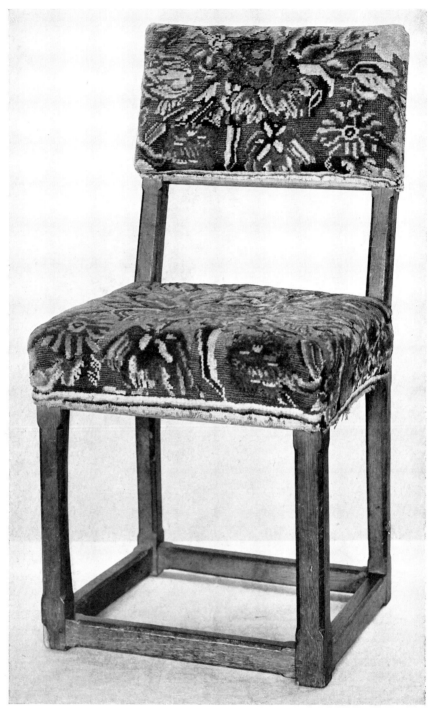

14. "Farthingale" Chair. Oak covered in "Turkey work". *Early* 17th century.

15. "Farthingale" Chair. Walnut. *Early* 17th century.

16. Walnut and beechwood. *1st half* of the 17th century.

17. Oak covered with "Turkey work". *Mid* 17th century.

18. Turned walnut covered in needlework. *Mid* 17th century.

19. Carved and turned oak, Lancashire type. *About* 1640–50.

20. Carved and turned oak, Lancashire type. *Dated* 1641.

21. Turned and carved oak, Yorkshire-Derbyshire type. *Mid* 17th century.

22. Carved and turned oak, Yorkshire-Derbyshire type. *Mid* 17th century.

23. Turned oak covered in leather. *About* 1650.

24. Carved and turned oak. *About* 1660.

25. Child's Arm-Chair. Carved, turned and inlaid oak. *About* 1625.

26. Child's Chair. Turned and carved oak. *Mid* 17th century.

27. Child's Chair. Turned walnut. *About* 1660–70.

28. Child's Chair. Carved and turned walnut. *About* 1685.

29. Chair-Table. Carved and turned oak. *About* 1650–60.

30. Turned walnut. *About* 1665.

31. Carved and turned walnut. *About* 1675.

32. Carved and turned walnut. *About* 1670–75.

33. Carved and turned walnut. *About* 1675.

34. Carved and pain
beechwood.
About 16

5. Carved walnut.
   About 1690.

36. Carved and painte
beechwood.
About 1690–9

. Carved and
rned walnut.
About 1675–80.

38. Turned walnut with adjustable back. *About* 1680.

39. A "Sleeping Chair". Carved and gilt. *About* 1675.

40. Gilt and painted. *About* 1675.

41. Carved and turned walnut, parcel gilt. *About* 1675.

42. Painted beechwood, parcel gilt. *About* 1685.

43. Carved and gilt. *About* 1680.

44. Japanned wood. *About* 1680.

45. Carved walnut. *About* 1690.

46. Carved walnut. *Early* 18th century.

47. Japanned beechwood. *About* 1710.

48. Wing Arm-Chair. Walnut covered in needlework. *About* 1700.

49. Turned beech, covered in Soho tapestry. *Early* 18th century.

50. Walnut covered in needlework. *About* 1715.

51. Carved and gilt. *About* 1715.

52. Carved and gilt beechwood. *About* 1717.

53. Carved walnut. *About* 1715.

54. Carved walnut. *About* 1720.

55. Carved walnut. *About* 1720–25.

56. "Writing-Chair". Carved walnut. *About* 1720.

57. "Gay's Writing-Chair". Mahogany. *About* 1720.

58. Carved walnut covered in gilt leather. *About* 1720.

59. Carved walnut. *About* 1725.

60. Carved mahogany. *About* 1730.

61. Carved and gilt wood. *About* 1725-30.

62. Walnut covered in needlework. *Mid* 18th century.

63. Carved mahogany. *About* 1740.

64. President's Chair. Carved, painted and gilt mahogany. *About* 1750.

65. Carved mahogany in "Gothic" style. *About* 1760–65.

66. Carved mahogany. *About* 1760.

67. Carved mahogany. *About* 1760.

68. Carved mahogany. *About* 1760.

69. Carved mahogany. *About* 1755.

70. Carved mahogany. *About* 1755.

71. Design from Chippendale's *Director*, 1754 (cf. No. 70).

72. "Ribband-Back" Arm-Chair. Carved mahogany. *About* 1755.

73. "Ribband-Back" Chair. Carved mahogany. *About* 1755.

74. "French" Arm-Chair. Carved mahogany. *About* 1760.

75. Carved mahogany in Chinese style. *About* 1755–60.

76. Parquetry of various woods. *About* 1760–65.

77. Carved mahogany. *About* 1765.

78. "Goldsmith's Chair". Windsor type. *Mid* 18th century.

79. Windsor Arm-Chair. Yew, in "Gothic" style. *Mid* 18th century.

80. "Cowper's Chair". Mahogany. *About* 1760–70.

81. Carved and gilt in neo-classic style. *About* 1765.

82. Carved and gilt. *About* 1777.

83. Design by Robert Adam, dated 1777.

84. Carved and gilt. *About* 1775.

85. Carved and gilt. *About* 1775.

86. President's Chair. Carved mahogany. *About* 1770.

87. "Lyre-Back" Chair. Carved mahogany. *About* 1775.

88. "Lyre-Back" Arm-Chair. Carved mahogany. *About* 1775.

89. "Lyre-Back" Arm-Chair. Various woods. *About* 1775.

90. "Lyre-Back" Arm-Chair. Carved mahogany. *About* 1775.

91. Painted beechwood. *About* 1775.

92. Painted beechwood. *About* 1776.

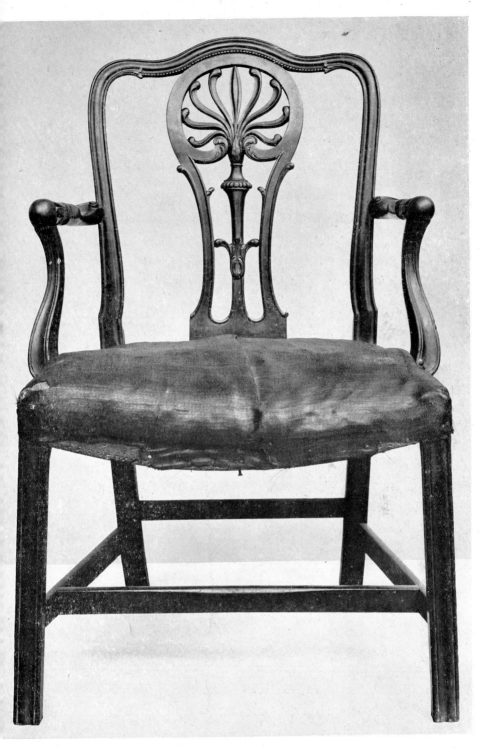

93. Carved mahogany. *About* 1770.

94. Ladder-Back Chair. Carved mahogany. *About* 1775.

95. Carved mahogany. *About* 1775.

96. Carved and inlaid mahogany. *About* 1775.

97. Carved mahogany. *About* 1775.

98. Carved and inlaid mahogany. *About* 1785.

99. Carved and turned mahogany. *About* 1785.

100. Carved mahogany, inset panel painted. *About* 1785.

101. Carved mahogany. *Dated* 1783.

102. Carved mahogany. *About* 1795.

102. Mahogany with painted decoration. *About* 1780–85.

104. Japanned beechwood. *About* 1790.

105. Painted satinwood. *About* 1790.

106. Japanned beechwood. *About* 1795.

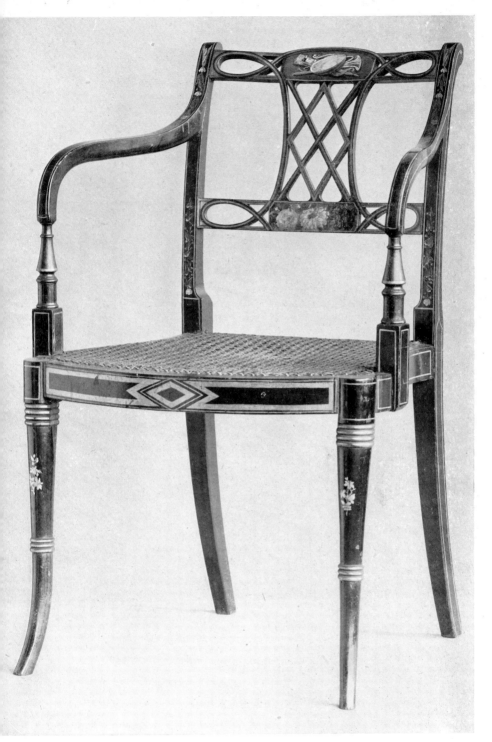

107. Japanned beechwood. *About* 1800.

108. Japanned beechwood. *About* 1800.

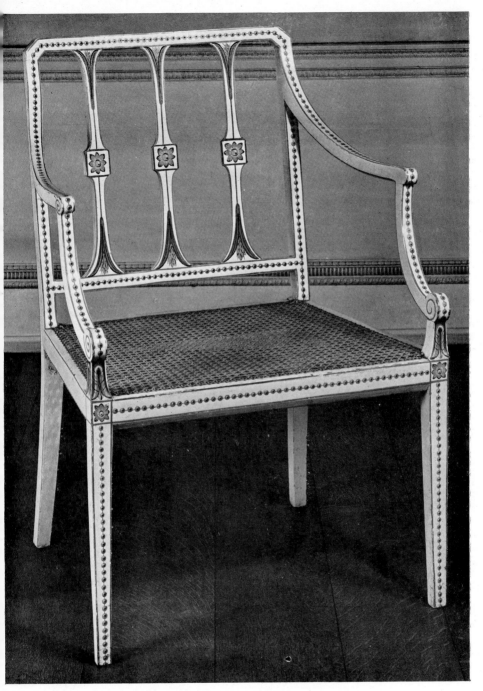

109. Painted beechwood. *About* 1790.

110. Hall-Chair. Painted beechwood. *About* 1775.

111. Hall-Chair. Carved mahogany. *About* 1800.

112. Various woods with brass stringing. *About* 1795–1800.

113. Japanned beechwood with brass mounts. *About* 1810.

114. Carved, painted and gilt wood. *About* 1810.

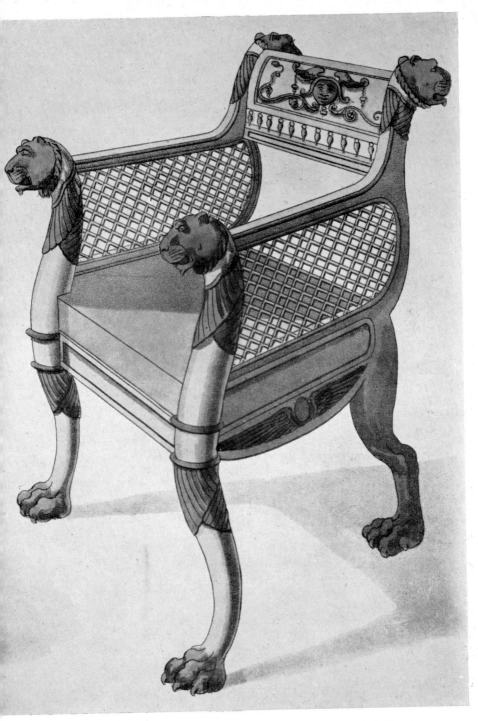

115. Design from George Smith's *Household Furniture* (1808).

116. Japanned and gilt beechwood. *About* 1810.

117. Stained beechwood. *About* 1810.

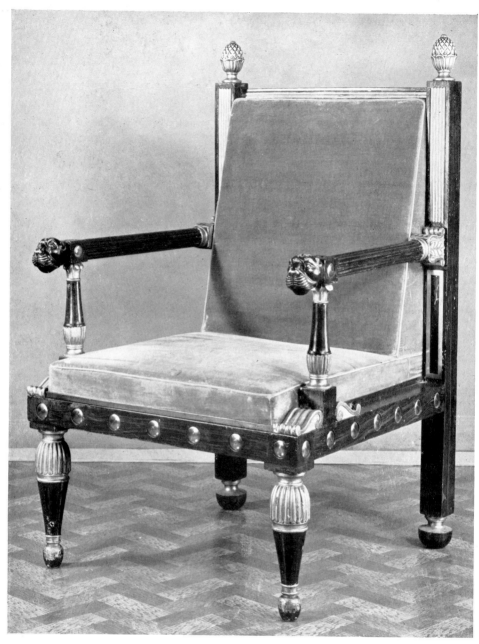

118. Carved, grained and parcel gilt. *About* 1807.

119. Mahogany inlaid with brass. *About* 1810–15.

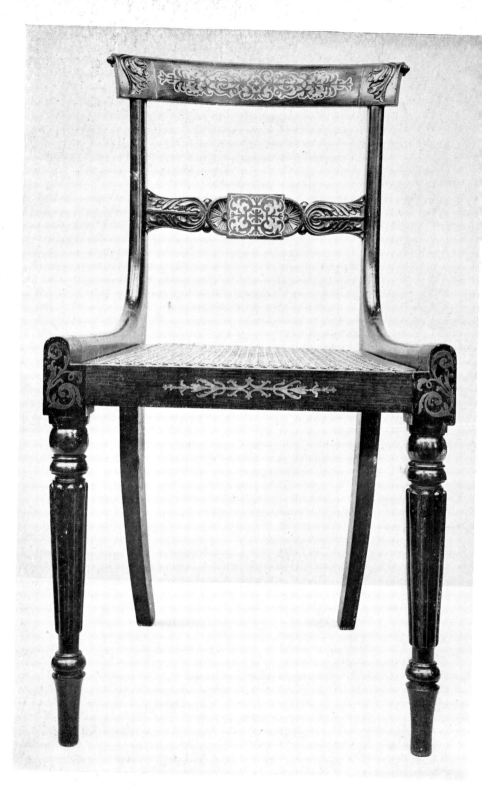

120. Beechwood and mahogany with brass inlay. *About* 1820.

Wt. 4078   K40   S.O. Code No. 29-1577*